Cost Accounting